Dear Reader,

Your feelings really matter. They matter to you and to those around you, so it's important to keep them fit and well! We keep our bodies healthy by exercising and eating good foods, but sometimes we forget that we should try to keep our minds healthy too. Taking care of our mental health helps us to look after our feelings and enjoy life.

Everyone has bad days – days when things just don't feel right. Maybe you feel grumpy, sad or just out of sorts. These are normal feelings and usually they pass. But sometimes an unpleasant feeling doesn't go away; instead it starts to grow. It may even grow so big that it squashes all your nice feelings. This is when you need to take action and find a way of being in charge of your feelings.

I hope that reading about how the young people in this book managed their feelings will help you if your feelings ever get on top of you. Of course, not everyone will experience the strong feelings that these young people have, but if you do, remember that you are not alone. Lots of children and adults experience difficult feelings, but that does not make them bad people! Like having a cold or a stomach bug, bad feelings can affect anyone and will usually go away by themselves. But if you, or a friend, have difficult feelings that don't go away it's best to tell a trusted adult, just as you would if someone had a temperature or was covered in a rash.

As for me, I try to keep healthy in mind and body by talking to my friends, getting enough sleep, exercising, eating well, meditating and trying to be kind to myself and others. Do I always succeed? Certainly not, but I keep trying!

Marcia

That's what friends are for!

Well, my feelings are private – I'm not sharing them with anyone!

You can always share them with us, because we're your friends.

For all the FANTASTIC children who contributed to this book.

Thank you, you made me feel so happy!

With thanks to our consultant psychologist Andrea Obholzer
for advising on the children's stories

WALKER BOOKS
AND SUBSIDIARIES
LONDON · BOSTON · SYDNEY · AUCKLAND

First published 2021 by Walker Books Ltd 87 Vauxhall Walk, London SE11 5HJ

This edition published 2022

2 4 6 8 10 9 7 5 3 1

© 2021 Marcia Williams

The right of Marcia Williams to be identified as author/illustrator of this work has been
asserted in accordance with the Copyright, Designs and Patents Act 1988

This book has been typeset in Puritan

Printed in China

All rights reserved. No part of this book may be reproduced, transmitted or stored in an
information retrieval system in any form or by any means, graphic, electronic or mechanical,
including photocopying, taping and recording, without prior written permission from the publisher.

British Library Cataloguing in Publication Data: a catalogue record for this book is available from the British Library

ISBN 978-1-5295-0409-5

www.walker.co.uk

Let's use this mood meter to check how we're feeling.

I'm putting myself here because Bertie's feeling fine. I'm not telling you how I feel.

I'm feeling excited because we're entering a new book!

angry   anxious   sad   shy   happy   proud   excited   jealous

We hope you enjoy this book.
Please return or renew it by the due date.
You can renew it at **www.norfolk.gov.uk/libraries**
or by using our free library app. Otherwise you can
phone **0344 800 8020** - please have your library
card and pin ready.
You can sign up for email reminders too.

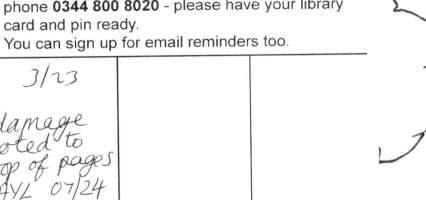

3/23

damage
noted to
top of pages
AYL 07/24

NORFOLK COUNTY COUNCIL
LIBRARY AND INFORMATION SERVICE

NORFOLK ITEM

3 0129 08798 7955

The FANTASTIC BOOK of FEELINGS

A Guide to Being Happy, Sad and Everything In-Between!

by Marcia Williams

Talking about my feelings makes me anxious. I think I might go home.

Oh, I love talking about my feelings, it makes me super happy!

Come on, Lou, we'll be with you — you can do this!

| angry | anxious | sad | shy | happy | proud | excited | jealous |

YOUR FANTASTIC FEELINGS!
ALL DIFFERENT – ALL GOOD

YOUR FEELINGS ARE FANTASTIC. They are unique to you and part of what makes you so special. Even feelings that you may find uncomfortable, like worry, sadness or anger, play a role in our lives. For instance, feeling anxious about being in the school play may help you focus on learning your lines!

There is no right or wrong way to feel, so we should never judge our feelings, or those of others. If we learn to understand our feelings, the happy ones, the angry ones and the sadder ones, then we can express them in positive ways that help us, and other people, enjoy life.

It is normal to experience different feelings throughout the day. Some will last a few seconds and others will be stronger and last longer. If a feeling grows so big you struggle to manage it on your own, talk to an adult you trust so they can help you. Because your feelings are special to you, even when you feel the same way about something as your friends, you may all react in a different way. Imagine six people all winning a prize – they will probably all feel happy, but that happiness may feel different for every winner. By learning to recognise and understand your feelings, you can find out ways to look after yourself, however you feel.

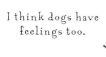

I think dogs have feelings too.

Yes, all animals have feelings.

Bertie always feels sad when you're unhappy, Lou.

And I feel sad when you are upset, Dot.

That's good, Lou, it means you are empathetic.

Empathy, or understanding others' feelings, is a great skill!

Woof!

TOP TEN TIPS –

1 BE KIND TO YOURSELF
Allow yourself to make mistakes and don't compare yourself to others. Be proud of your own achievements.

2 TAKE REGULAR EXERCISE
Find a sport that suits you and enjoy it! It can be anything: walking, football, swimming, rock climbing, dancing. Whatever it is, it will make you feel good!

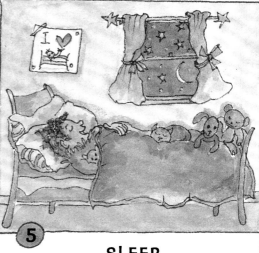

3 EAT WELL
Eating a balanced diet with lots of fruit, vegetables and fish (unless you're a vegetarian) can help to boost your mental health.

4 A GRATITUDE JAR
Write down things you're grateful for and pop them in a jar to remind you of all the good things in your life.

5 SLEEP
Not getting enough sleep is bad for your mental and physical health. Regular bedtimes and no screens in bed will help you settle better.

You may never entirely understand why you get certain feelings, but you can learn to recognise them, which will help you make better choices. If you notice that you feel uncomfortable taking part in a certain activity, you can find an activity that makes you feel happier. Learning about your feelings will also help you recognise when a friend is feeling down and needs extra support from you. Even if you are one of those lucky people who feel happy and positive every day, it is important to realise that other people don't always feel the same as you.

FOR KEEPING YOUR FEELINGS FIT!

6 RELAX

Find a hobby you enjoy. Woodwork, painting, singing, dancing – whatever it is, being absorbed in a task you love is very relaxing.

Would you like a lolly?

7 DO A KIND DEED

Share your sweets or just give someone a smile. A small act of kindness can change your mood for the day – and make the other person happier too!

How are you feeling today?

8 TALK TO SOMEONE

Talking to people about how you feel can stop uncomfortable feelings from getting too big for you to manage. Besides, it's great to spend time with friends and family!

9 READ A BOOK

Reading can take you into a different world and give you a chance to escape from your feelings for a while.

Knock, knock!

Who's there?

Boo!

10 WATCH A FUNNY MOVIE OR TELL A JOKE

Laughter is a great way to help keep your feelings fit and share time with your friends!

You may be feeling fine today, but feelings are for life so it is good to explore some different ways of keeping them fit and well. This will help you to remain in charge of your feelings, instead of them taking charge of you. You don't have to be feeling sad, angry or anxious to start looking after your feelings. The ideas on this page have all been shown to help our mental well-being, whether we're young, old, or in the middle. Some will work for you better than others, so it's fine to pick the ones that suit you best. If you want to keep your fantastic feelings fit, give them a go!

What stories, Dot?

Special stories about children and their feelings.

Shall we turn the page and read about Alisha? She felt anxious, like you Lou, until ... well, let's see.

FEELING ANXIOUS

You will definitely have felt anxious at some point in your life. Anxiety is that nervous feeling you sometimes get before you meet new people, perform in a school play, or take a test. Some people just get butterflies in their stomach, but others feel so anxious their life feels out of their control. Anxiety may give them sweaty palms, make it difficult to sleep, or even make them feel unable to move or speak. Sometimes, anxiety can be useful, like when it encourages you to revise for a test so you feel less worried about it! But it's not helpful if, like Alisha, you feel anxious most of the time, even when there's nothing in particular you are worrying about. Alisha could always find something to worry about, which was exhausting and stopped her from enjoying life.

ALISHA'S STORY

Mum says that I was born anxious! But all I remember about way back then is hating Mum and Dad going out and leaving me with a babysitter. I always worried that they would never come back!

As I grew older there just seemed more things to feel anxious about, and my list of worries grew and grew.

By the time I was seven my tummy was nearly always full of butterflies in heavy boots – even when I went to bed.

Before I could go to sleep, I had to wash my hands three times, check that every teddy was in the right place and make sure nobody turned out the light.

When my granny came to stay for my birthday, I felt anxious that she'd think I was weird. But she just hugged me and cooked me my favourite foods.

ALISHA'S TOP TIP:

Try meditating – even a really short meditation can calm your anxiety!

So Lou, what are you going to do now when you feel anxious?

I'm going to close my eyes and take three deep breaths, letting them out with a big sigh.

That's great Lou! Or you could try squeezing and opening your fists to the count of three.

At night, Granny read me my story. She smiled as I checked my teddies, washed my hands three times and insisted that she left the light on.

Granny said that she was a worrier too, and that even catching the train to visit me had made her so anxious she'd almost been sick – but then she did her meditation exercises!

BREATHING IN   **SIGHING OUT**

Granny asked me to lie on the floor beside her, close my eyes and take three deep breaths through my nose, letting each one out slowly with a loud sigh.

SQUEEZE TIGHT   **OPEN SLOWLY**

Granny also showed me how to focus on squeezing my fists tightly for the count of three – and then slowly opening them again, like the petals of a flower.

I felt sad when Granny went home, but I kept doing the meditations. Sometimes, Mum, Dad or my teddies did them too. After a while, I realised that I was going to bed without tidying my teddies or washing my hands – it felt amazing! I still get anxious now and then and have to tidy my teddies or check under the bed for monsters, but now I know what to do. Even when I feel anxious at school, I can do a little meditation exercise. I just close my eyes and take three deep breaths, or tense and relax my hands under my desk. Nobody even knows I'm doing it and it helps the bad moment pass. I can do lots of things now that used to make me anxious, but going to parties is the best!

FEELING SAD

Not feeling happy all the time is a normal part of life. Sometimes sad feelings creep up on you for no particular reason, and then just vanish again. At other times you might feel sad because something has gone wrong – someone has been unkind, a pet is ill, or a loved one has died. Or maybe, like Georgie, a best friend has gone away just when you are about to go into a new class at school. When this happened to Georgie he woke up each morning with a hollow feeling in his tummy. It felt like hunger, but it was sadness. Georgie stopped wanting to eat, go to school, or play with his other friends. The feeling of sadness was stopping Georgie doing things that he usually enjoyed.

GEORGIE'S STORY

I'm at primary school now, but Joe has been my best friend since our first day at preschool. So when Joe went to live in Australia I felt really sad.

I didn't want to eat.

I didn't want to play.

I couldn't sleep.

Mostly, I shut myself in my bedroom and played video games. They stopped me thinking about being sad.

Starting a new school year with a new teacher and no Joe was tough. I just wanted to stay at home.

GEORGIE'S TOP TIP:

Share your sad feeling with a trusted adult or friend.

Sometimes, I think my sad feelings are too silly to share – people might laugh.

Why not whisper them to me and Abe? We'd never laugh at you.

I get a really bad sad feeling when I think about all the wildlife that's struggling in my neighbourhood.

I didn't think my new teacher would understand why I felt sad. She suggested writing it down to put in the Worry Box.

This is what I wrote.

The next day I visited Mandy, our school counsellor. She had read my note. We talked a lot about Joe, which made me feel better.

After that I saw Mandy most days. Dad came to see her too and said he missed Joe's dad, just like I was missing Joe!

Dad and I started talking about Joe and his dad a lot, and sometimes we phoned them. It made us both feel better.

Mum signed me up for the Gardening Club, which is run by Miss Megan, my old teacher. I planted rows of carrots in Joe's honour, because he loved a carrot. The rest of Gardening Club thought I was nuts, but it made us all laugh! Mum also encouraged me to join the football club. I went to please her, but now I've made a new friend there, called Pete, so I like it. I still miss Joe and sometimes I need a hug from Mum or a chat with Mandy. But now if I feel sad I know that shutting myself in my room is not the answer.

We could plant a wildlife garden, would that help?

That's a brilliant idea, Dot. I'm so glad I shared my sad feeling with you.

From now on, I'll always share my sad feelings with you Dot, because you might know just how to help.

FEELING JEALOUS

Do you ever wish you had as many toys as your friends, could eat as many sweets or stay up as late as them? Jealousy is that feeling of envy. You may feel jealous of a brother or sister because you suspect your parents favour them, or you may get jealous when a friend plays with someone other than you, because it makes you worry they won't need you as a friend any more. Jealousy is often known as "the green-eyed monster" and is not a pleasant feeling, as Tommy found out. Tommy lived with a foster family, and was very happy until they invited Mia to join them for Christmas, then Tommy began to feel extremely jealous.

TOMMY'S STORY

I have lived with my foster family for three years. There's Sonia, Dave, little Paul, Brutus the dog, the ponies and me.

Just before last Christmas, my social worker asked Sonia and Dave if they would look after Mia.

They rushed out to buy extra presents for Mia. Then Dave made his famous glitter cake to welcome her.

You'd have thought she was a princess, the fuss everyone made of her.

On Christmas morning we opened our presents. I noticed that Mia had two more than me.

TOMMY'S TOP TIP:

Try to do something nice with or for the person you're jealous of.

I used to be jealous of my little brother and pinch him! Now, I play with him instead.

I feel jealous when you two play together and leave me out. I think you don't like me.

I'm glad you told us that, next time we'll ask you to join in.

We had pancakes for breakfast and Mia got the last one.

Then Mia offered to help feed the ponies, which was my job.

I hated Mia being there. Even Brutus was ignoring me and fussing over her.

I went to my room and slammed the door firmly shut.

Dave came and knocked on my door. He asked me if I could help make Mia feel at home.

He reminded me of how I'd felt when I first arrived to live with them.

Eventually, Dave persuaded me to go downstairs and try to help make Mia feel part of the family. Once I stopped thinking about how cross I was that Mia was there, I began to feel better, and soon we were both laughing at Dave's silly jokes. We played games, pulled crackers and I showed Mia Brutus' tickling spot, how Paul liked to ride on my back and that I could eat five mince pies in one sitting! Although I still felt the odd twinge of jealousy, like when Mia cried for her mum and Sonia gave her a cuddle, doing things with Mia made me feel so much better. It also made me realise that Mia deserved a happy Christmas just like me!

It feels so much nicer being kind to someone, instead of being jealous of them.

It's not always easy though.

We'll just have to practise lots!

Woof!

FEELING SHY

There is nothing wrong with feeling shy. Some people just seem to be born shy, but nearly everyone feels a little shy now and then. Maybe you feel shy when you meet new people, or have to speak in class. When you feel shy you might blush, feel a bit shaky or not want to speak. Shyness only becomes a problem when it stops you saying or doing the things you would like to. Ella felt so shy, she was unable to make friends or join in activities with other children. It wasn't that she didn't want to, but she couldn't find a way to overcome her shyness.

ELLA'S STORY

I live in a large old house with Mum, Dad, my three brothers and two sisters. I am the baby of the family, nicknamed Snaily because I have always been shy and wanted to hide away – like a snail in its shell!

Even at home I only spoke when my magic bunny toy was close by.

At school, I would sit on top of the climbing frame and watch the other children play.

I wanted to be friends with Mandy, but I was too shy to ask.

Mandy was brilliant at cartwheels and back flips.

I was good at them too, but only in my bedroom!

Then one day Mandy joined me on the climbing frame. She was crying.

ELLA'S TOP TIP:

Set yourself goals and celebrate when you achieve them!

That's such good advice.

But you never feel shy, Abe.

He feels shy when he talks to adults.

After break Mandy was meant to do her show and tell, but she felt shy and didn't want to do it!

I had never dreamed that somebody as popular as Mandy might be shy too. I was so astonished I actually spoke to her!

Mandy had planned to show the class how to do a cartwheel, but she was sure she'd make a mess of it.

We decided to do it together. I felt so nervous I couldn't speak, but Mandy spoke and I did the cartwheel – everyone cheered!

GOALS

Smile at the postman.

Ask a question in class.

Ask Mandy for a sleepover.

Ask my family to stop calling me Snaily!

Since then Mandy and I have been best friends. I never feel shy when it's just the two of us. I still feel shy in front of lots of people, particularly with adults. But I try to do something new and brave every day, like putting my hand up in class or smiling at someone I don't know. I still carry my bunny around, just to give me courage – you might think it's babyish, but he just makes me feel better. Even on the days I forget him and he stays at home! I think I'll always feel a bit shy, but if I keep practising I'm sure I'll eventually pop right out of my shell and nobody will call me Snaily ever again!

I think we all feel a little shy at times.

My goal is to say hello to Mum and Dad's friends when they visit.

That's a great goal, I think Bertie and I might try that too.

FEELING FEAR

Everyone feels fear sometimes. You might have a fear of snakes, thunderstorms, scary movies, or even something imagined. Fear makes your heart beat faster and your muscles tense, preparing you to fight off the danger, or run away from it. As we get older we learn to calm our fears by understanding the level of danger we face. But sometimes, like Ronnie, we develop a fear of something which starts to cause us problems in our everyday lives. Ronnie had never been bitten by a dog, or even growled at by one, but he was sure that every dog was just waiting for a chance to attack him. He wished he was braver, but even the smallest dog made his legs turn to jelly!

RONNIE'S STORY

I live with my mum in a caravan by the sea. It would be the best place in the world, if it wasn't for the dogs! Everyone seems to have a dog except for us, because I've always been scared of dogs – really, really scared.

Holiday makers sit on the beach with dogs.

Elderly ladies push little dogs in prams!

Caravaners tie dogs to their steps outside.

Campers sleep on the beach with dogs.

I'm always in trouble for being late for school. I have to cross the road so many times to avoid passing too close to a dog.

Then, one summer the very worst thing happened: my mum invited my cousin Joe and his puppy Lola to stay!

RONNIE'S TOP TIP:

Take small steps to face your fear!

Do you have any fears that need facing, Lou?

You'll think my fear is really stupid – it's falling in a muddy puddle that has no bottom.

No fear is stupid, Abe.

The night before they arrived I dreamt that Lola bit me!

In the morning I felt sick and had to stay in bed.

When Joe knocked on the door, my heart beat louder than the knocker.

Luckily, Lola was in a travel crate, so Joe left her and we went out to play – until a huge dog tried to get our ball.

That afternoon I took Joe rock-pooling. We found a big crab. Joe screamed and Lola popped her head out of his T-shirt. She had been with us all along!

After that, Lola just hung out with us, which was OK as long as she didn't touch me. At night Lola slept on Joe's bed, but on their last night I woke to find Lola lying on my feet! My heart was racing. We stared at each other, then Lola rolled over and went back to sleep. I actually fell back asleep too … with a dog on my bed!

I felt really proud when I woke up the next day, and quite sad that Joe was leaving. I think that getting to know Lola, bit by bit, made me realise that I can handle my fear. My heart still pounds when I see an enormous dog, but I don't run away and I haven't been late for school for six weeks, which is definitely a Ronnie record!

I can't swim and I think I may sink under the water.

Well, next time it rains we'll face that fear together.

Little splash by little splash!

FEELING HATE

Most of us like some people more than others, and also dislike some people more than others. We might dislike a classmate who bullies us, an adult who has treated us unfairly, or even a sibling. Usually, this feeling of dislike will pass. But sometimes, it turns into a boiling hot feeling inside you, which we call hate. Hating somebody doesn't make you a bad person, but it's not a good feeling and can make you and the person you hate miserable. Amber found this out when she began to hate her younger brother, Harrison.

AMBER'S STORY

I was three when my little brother Harrison arrived, and I was really pleased. I loved helping my dads look after him, and he always had a smile for me.

But as he grew older he got really annoying. He messed with my things, and never let me play by myself.

Even if I had a friend over for tea or for a sleepover, Harrison would barge into my room and annoy us!

It didn't matter how nicely I asked him, he just never gave me any space – not even to do my homework!

One day when I told him to go away, he bit my arm and kicked my toys across the room. I boiled over.

AMBER'S TOP TIP:

Make a list of things that are annoying you about someone and talk to a friend or family member.

I'd talk to you and Dot if I needed to.

I used to hate my teacher because I thought she was always picking on me.

I remember, but after you and your mum talked to her things got better.

I pushed him out of my room and slammed the door in his face. Harrison screamed and screamed!

Dad Dave heard the racket and came leaping up the stairs, two at a time. He took Harrison down to the kitchen.

After some quiet time on my own, I began to feel better, and my hate for Harrison wasn't quite so fierce.

I went down for supper and asked my dads if I could have a lock on my door to keep Harrison out.

Amber

Help Harrison with his reading, so he can read your signs!

Never touch Harrison's toys without asking.

Put a positive thought about Harrison in the Friendship Jar every week.

If you want to hit Harrison, go and hit your pillows.

Spend time playing with Harrison.

Put a penny in the charity box every time you call Harrison a rude name.

Use kind words or say nothing!

Harrison

Always knock on Amber's door – or do her chores.

Never touch Amber's toys without asking.

Think of a nice thing to say to Amber when she comes back from school.

If you want to bite Amber, bite your teddy instead.

Put a penny in the charity box every time you call Amber a rude name.

Use kind words or zip your mouth.

My dads said I could have ice cream for pudding, even though I'd been rude and cross, but I could not have a lock on my door, because that would be dangerous. After supper we made a list of reasons why Harrison and I hated each other, and another list of what to do about it. My favourite is that Harrison has to knock on my door – always – or do my Saturday chores! He also has to leave me alone, if I ask him nicely. Harrison likes our friendship jar best, because he likes seeing how cool I think he is – which I mostly do as long as he never, ever touches my things without my permission. I'm not perfect, I still hate him sometimes – but mostly I don't!

Hate sounds like a really BIG feeling.

Yes, it makes your insides boil and your head feel like splitting!

Hate is a negative feeling, that's why you hate it! It's good to avoid it if you can.

FEELiNG LONELY

Being alone is not the same as feeling lonely – we all like to have time alone sometimes. There are also things that might make you feel a bit lonely, like moving to a new house, or being unwell and missing your friends. Whatever the reason, the feeling usually goes away quite quickly. But if the feeling stays, as it did for Kate, it can make you so sad that you stop bothering to make friends, or doing the things you usually enjoy. Kate's mother had died when she was little and she lived alone with her dad. They got on really well, but when he was busy Kate felt lonely. This lonely feeling began to follow her to school. Kate would stand at the edge of the playground, not wanting to join in, but not really wanting to be on her own.

KATE'S STORY

> You chop and I'll cook.

> No babe, you chop and I'll cook.

> And what will I do?

I love my dad, he's super cool, but sometimes I got lonely at home. Like when Dad and his girlfriend Sally cooked supper together. Also, Dad works really hard writing books, and when he shut his study door I'd feel lonely.

> 1, 2, 3…

I began to feel lonely at school too. There was a skipping craze …

> Why don't you join in?

> I'm not good at skipping, Miss.

… but I can't skip. I watched the other kids but couldn't join in.

> My mum helped me make it.

> Yeah, mine too.

After skipping it was the slime craze, but I hated the stuff!

> Kate's in charge today. Take your books to her.

> Please, Kate, can you help me read this?

> Of course, this is one of my favourites!

One day, my teacher Miss Primmer asked me to help in the library at break time. I didn't want to, but I soon found I enjoyed helping the little kids read and choose their books. It was better than skipping and a lot better than slime.

KATE'S TOP TIP:

Try something new, so that you meet people who have the same interests as you.

That's a good tip, everything changed for Kate when she started helping in the library.

You could join a club, where you might make new friends.

Excellent idea, Lou. Or you could start your own club – Kate could start a book club!

When I told Dad he asked if I ever felt lonely at home. I didn't want to upset him, but eventually I admitted that I did.

He was a little upset that I hadn't told him before, because mums and dads like to help if we have a problem.

Now Dad never, ever shuts the door to his study and I'm even allowed to do my homework in there.

When Sally comes round we all cook together, which is fun and a little chaotic.

I still help in the library some days, because I've made lots of reading friends. They even come and find me in the playground. I'm glad Miss Primmer asked me to help. I can still remember that sick feeling of loneliness in my stomach, but it's mostly a memory. If I feel it creeping back, I know I can ask Dad for a cuddle, or invite a book friend over to tea. I'm also secretly trying to learn some slime and skipping skills, but don't tell anyone because I'm not ready to go public quite yet!

I think it was very brave of Kate to help in the library.

Yes, it was and it really helped her make loads of new friends.

I think it's good to have friends of all ages too, then you get to share their different interests.

FEELING ANGRY

Never feeling angry would be impossible. Sometimes things happen that you can't help but feel angry about. Maybe someone in your family is annoying you, maybe you have too much homework, or your best friend is ignoring you. Perhaps your team lost a game, or somebody has treated you, or a friend, unfairly. Whatever it is, anger can be a natural reaction. When you're angry you may start to breathe faster, clench your fists, go red in the face, yell or even want to hit something or someone! Anger can be helpful if it makes you realise that something is wrong and that you need to change it. But if your anger explodes in a bad way, like Charlie's did, then you need to find ways of calming yourself down until the feeling passes.

CHARLIE'S STORY

Come on, Charlie, you'll be late for school.

I don't even want to go to school and somebody's taken my tie!

Sometimes, I'd wake up with a cross feeling in the pit of my stomach and I would just know it was going to be a bad, angry day.

That's my cereal, I hate you.

Charlie, calm down.

If my sister Lily had finished my favourite cereal I would definitely yell at her!

I don't want toast, I want my cereal!

If Mum offered me toast instead of my cereal, my anger would grow hotter and noisier.

It's my turn to go in the front!

Get in, or walk.

I'd start to feel as though I was in the middle of a raging storm.

You stink!

Charlie, don't be so rude!

By the time I got to school, I would be too angry to work and far too angry to be nice to my friends. I'm a kind person really, so it didn't feel good.

Goal to Tom!

Serves you right, idiot!

What did I do?

Charlie, go and sit outside the school office this instant!

At break time if someone other than me scored a goal in our football match I would explode. Once, I even pulled my best friend Tom's hair, landing him face down on the ground!

CHARLIE'S TOP TIP:

Close your eyes and let your mind travel to its very own calm place.

Does that mean that you pretend to be somewhere else, somewhere special to you?

Yes. You love the seaside, so you could imagine you're playing on a beach.

I'd imagine I was running a marathon and everyone was cheering for me!

I was in BIG trouble after that. The headteacher gave me some bubble wrap to snap, while we waited for my mum and dad to arrive.

Mum was upset, but Dad said he'd been like me when he was younger: always wanting to be first, be on top, be the winner.

I must be just like Dad, because that's exactly how I feel. I feel rubbish if I I'm not the winner, even if it's just winning the last bowl of cereal!

The headteacher said he'd let it go this time, but I needed to talk to Mum and Dad about how to control my anger, because next time he might have to exclude me from school!

Mum, Dad, Lily and I had a long talk that night. We thought of all the things that make us angry. Mum said it was when nobody helps her with the washing-up, Lily said it was when I play with her toys, Dad said he gets furious when people call him a grump! Lots of things make me angry, but mostly it's when I feel rubbish at something and don't come first. We each made a list of things we could do to help us calm down when we feel angry. Now I try really hard not to explode but to do something from my list. My favourite thing is hugging the dog, my least favourite is star jumps! I still erupt like a volcano sometimes – but nobody is perfect, not even a winner like me!

WHAT MAKES YOU HAPPY?

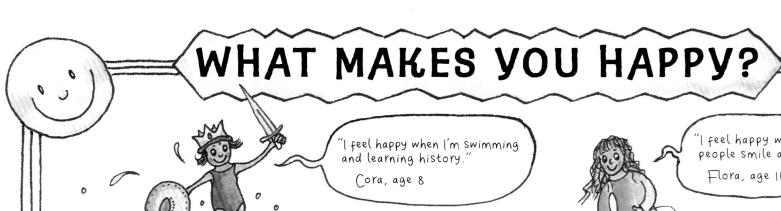

"I feel happy when I'm swimming and learning history."

Cora, age 8

"I feel happy when people smile at me."

Flora, age 10

"Football and eating spaghetti bolognese for dinner both make me feel happy!"

Jesse, age 10

"I feel happy when I am around my friends, family and my cat or doing something I enjoy. I am most happy when I am on holiday in France."

Cecily, age 16

"I feel happy when I'm with my friends."

May, age 6

"When we have banana splits for pudding, with all the yummy cream and ice cream, I feel really happy. Riding my bike also makes me happy, because the whooshing wind is fun and wears me out."

Ranulph, age 7

"It can depend. Obviously personal hobbies like theatre and politics bring me a lot of joy. On the whole, I think kindness goes a long way to making me feel happy. People just being nice to others is what mainly gives me happiness."

Paul, age 16

Happiness is really important to all of us, so it is a good idea to try to work out what makes you happy. When you're happy it helps you make others feel happy, and it gives you the chance to make the most of your opportunities. Happiness can feel like a small, calm little glow inside you, a quiet voice that tells you all's right with your world. Or it can burst out of you and make you want to sing and dance and hug everybody! Some people feel like that every day and hardly even notice the feeling, it is so much a part of them. Other people really have to work at feeling happy. Both are quite normal and if you do have to work at happiness that's fine, because there are loads of ways to do that.

I agree with Paul, kindness makes me happy ... and baking cupcakes!

I'm with Flora, smiles make me happy.

Being kind and smiling at other people can make both you and them feel happy!

"When I'm happy I like to laugh a lot. The things that make me giggle are playing with my brother Louis on the trampoline, my dad's whiskers, my mum pretending to fall asleep and snore on me, and my brother Max letting me put clips and bows in his hair!"

Honor, age 8

"Seeing my dog makes me happy."

Delphi, age 10

"I feel happy when I'm with my friends and family, especially when I'm laughing with them."

Mathilda, age 14

"My pets, Fluffy and Scratch, make me feel happy."

Ava, age 10

"Walking in the woods, snuggling under a duvet and watching a film, and spending time with other people makes me happy."

David, age 7

"Playing with my cat Tinky; chatting and playing with my friends; baking; having time with my mum; having sleepovers; playing with my brother; going on holiday as I like exploring and meeting people; watching TV, all makes me happy."

Esme, age 10

"My friends, my family and horses make me feel happy!"

May, age 13

"Running, football, cycling and playing with my cars and Lego all make me happy."

Rex, age 8

"I feel happy when I'm eating roast potatoes."

Thom, age 6

Just look at all the different things that help to make these children feel happy. You might like to try some of them. None of them mention having loads of stuff, or being wealthy, so it won't cost you anything! Happiness is a feeling that comes from mental well-being. Of course, it is different for everyone, but there does seem to be one thing that helps most of us to feel happy and that is friendship and family. It appears that we are happiest when we are sharing time with people we like, love or feel comfortable with, either just hanging out, or doing things like exercising, playing music or being creative together. You might like to make a list of things that make you happy.

I think that I make Bertie happy just by being me.

Woof, woof!

You do make me laugh, Lou. But that laughter makes me feel happy!

Just hanging out with you guys makes me feel happy ... and Thom's roasties!

FIRST AID BOX

Most days are fairly ordinary, but now and then you might be unlucky and hurt yourself. If you do, you don't ignore your injury. You go and find first aid to stop the injury getting worse. In the same way, if something upsets you and causes difficult feelings that stay around for too long and grow too big, you need to seek first aid. Nobody goes through life without the odd cut and bruise, and nobody goes through life without a few difficult feelings!

The children in this book all discovered ways to help themselves when they felt their feelings getting too big – and you can too! You may never need to use this first aid box, but it is good to know it's there and what's inside it. Then if you, or a friend, can't manage your feelings on your own, you will have some remedies at the ready. Over time, you will discover what works best for you and then you can create your own first aid box. In the meantime, remember that the very best first aid for feelings is to share them with a trusted adult.

- FEELING ANXIOUS -

- Don't ignore your anxiety, think about what's causing it. Is there something you're feeling nervous about? Is there anything you can do to prepare for it that would help your nerves?

- Try to be brave and face your anxiety. Talk about it, draw a picture of it, write about it. The more you express it, the less anxious it may make you feel.

- Do some exercise to help relax your body.

- If anxiety is stopping you sleeping, try doing some breathing exercises in bed. Imagine your breath is going in through your nose, down to your toes and then up and out again. Keep doing this until you drift off to sleep.

- FEELING SHY -

- Remember that everyone feels shy sometimes. You are not alone.

- If you have a skill or hobby, try to share it with other people. It's easier to talk to people if it's about something you're really interested in.

- Remember, there is nothing wrong with feeling shy, it only matters if it is stopping you joining in with your friends.

- Join a drama club. Performing is a great way to build up your confidence.

- If you feel shy of adults, you can always practise some things to talk about with a parent or guardian.

- FEELING ANGRY -

- Take some time out and walk away from whatever is causing your anger.

- Take three deep breaths in, and as you breathe out let your whole body go floppy and relaxed.

- Count to ten and if that doesn't work, count to ten again!

- Take a mind holiday. Shut your eyes and imagine you're doing something that you really love. Keep this visual image in your First Aid Box so that it's always there when you need it.

- Try to explain your anger, but never hurt someone physically or with your words.

- FEELING SAD -

- Talk to someone you trust about what's making you sad – don't be alone.

- Write about your sadness in a journal, or draw a picture.

- Listen to your favourite music.

- Do some exercise, even just going for a walk can really help improve your feelings, especially if you do it with friends or family.

- Give your parent or a friend a cuddle – we all need cuddles and they can help us feel less sad.

- Have a good cry – there are times to be brave and times to let those tears roll!

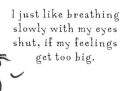

I just like breathing slowly with my eyes shut, if my feelings get too big.

Me too, it's so calming. I like drawing how I feel too.

Your breath is like a friend who is always there for you.

FOR FEELINGS!

- FEELING HATE -

- Feeling hatred for someone is often a mixed emotion, so it is helpful to look at why you have that feeling. Maybe you are jealous of the person, or angry because they have treated you unfairly. Knowing why you feel as you do will help you take control of the feeling.
- Try to understand the person you hate. It may help you realise why they are behaving in a way that upsets you.
- Talk to someone about your feelings. If the person you hate is bullying you, tell a trusted adult.
- Listen to music, read a book or play a video game to give your feelings time to calm down.

- FEELING JEALOUS -

- Try to work out why you feel jealous. Knowing why you feel something often helps you work out ways to cope with that feeling.
- Get to know the person you're jealous of. It might help you see that you don't need to feel jealous of them.
- Try to accept that life is not fair. Some people will always have things that you can't have.
- Keep a gratitude jar or journal to remind yourself of how much there is to be happy about.
- Be kinder to yourself and acknowledge all your good points.

- FEELING LONELY -

- Join a group like the Scouts, or a school club, so that you can meet new people.
- Become a pen friend to a child in another country, or to a relative.
- Volunteer for something, either at school or at home.
- Start a new hobby, or practise a new skill which you can share with others.
- If you are having to stay at home from school because you are unwell, think about catching up with your friends by email or on the phone.

- FEELING FEAR -

- Take some deep breaths when you're facing your fear.
- Write, draw or talk about your fear. It will help you understand your feeling better.
- Keep a fear diary, noting down every time you feel scared and whether anything you did helped to calm your fear.
- Try to face up to your fears. They won't go away if you avoid them, but if you confront them gradually they may prove not to be as bad as you thought. Ask an adult or friend to support you.

- IF YOUR FRIEND HAS DIFFICULT FEELINGS -

- Listen to how they are feeling with your full attention. Being a good listener is a great skill.
- Take them seriously. However silly their feeling may seem to you, it's very real to them.
- Be a trustworthy friend by not sharing what they've told you with other people, unless it is with a trusted adult.
- Let them know they are not alone and that you have feelings that are hard to manage too sometimes.
- Offer to do something with them, like going for a bike ride or a walk. Exercise can help calm difficult feelings.
- Encourage them to tell an adult if their feelings are too strong for them to manage.

Remember: **Never be ashamed or embarrassed by your feelings. Everybody has both weird and wonderful feelings – you are not alone!**

Bertie likes to take some exercise when his feelings get too big.

Well, that's good. The important thing is to find out what works for you.

Then you've always got a feelings plaster at the ready!

iNDEX

celebrate the things you're good at

look at what you've achieved, not what you've failed to do

make a mood meter

do some gardening

play team sports

watch a funny film

Here are some more ideas to help you with your feelings.

Spend time with people who make you feel good, not bad.

Give someone a hug!

angry   anxious   sad   shy   happy   proud   excited   jealous

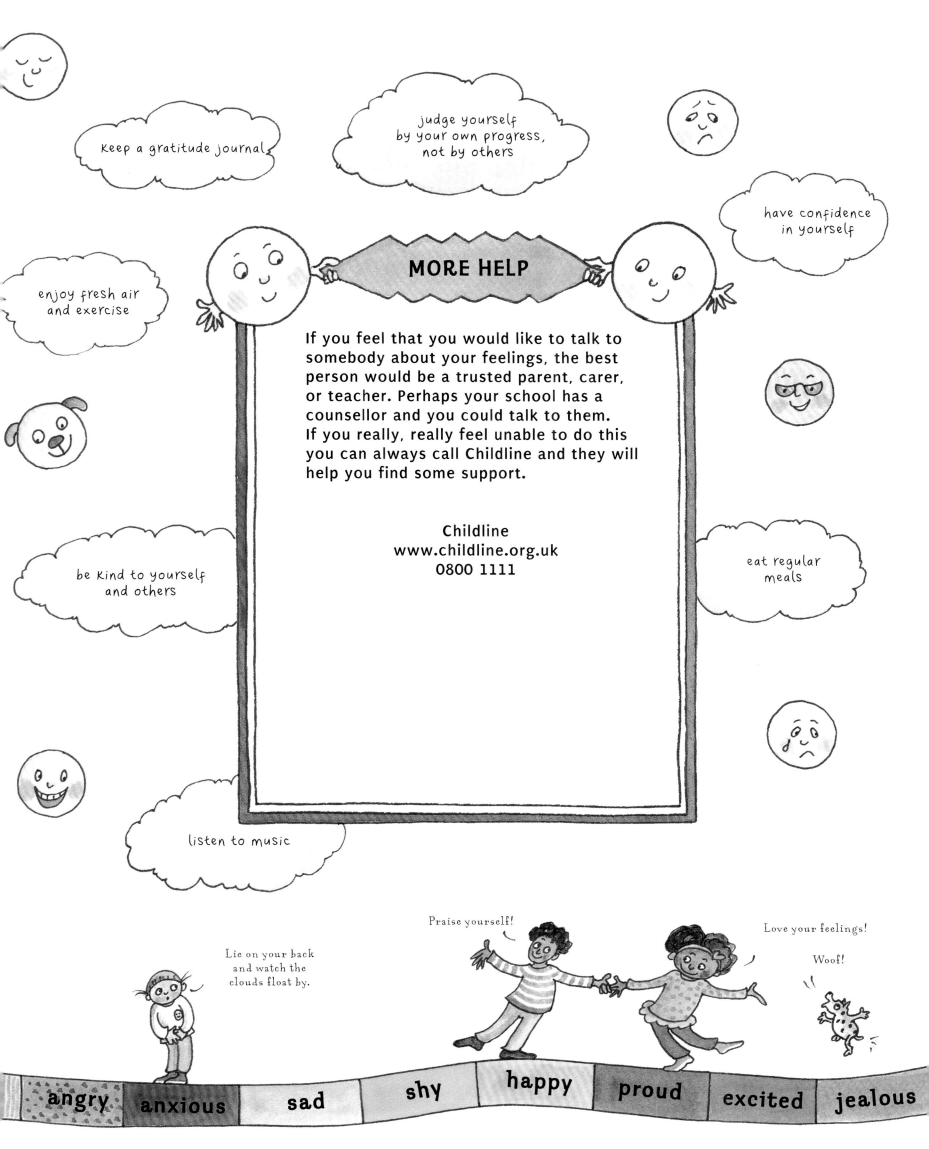

Keep a gratitude journal

judge yourself by your own progress, not by others

have confidence in yourself

enjoy fresh air and exercise

MORE HELP

If you feel that you would like to talk to somebody about your feelings, the best person would be a trusted parent, carer, or teacher. Perhaps your school has a counsellor and you could talk to them. If you really, really feel unable to do this you can always call Childline and they will help you find some support.

Childline
www.childline.org.uk
0800 1111

be kind to yourself and others

eat regular meals

listen to music

Lie on your back and watch the clouds float by.

Praise yourself!

Love your feelings!

Woof!

| angry | anxious | sad | shy | happy | proud | excited | jealous |

MARCIA WILLIAMS

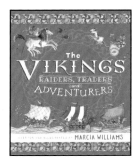

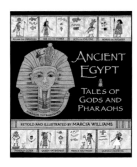

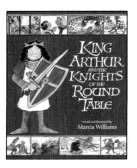

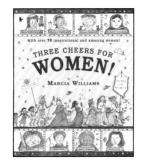

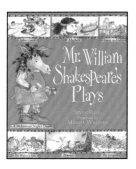
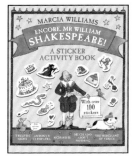

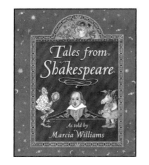

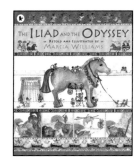
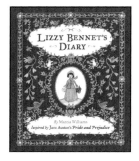

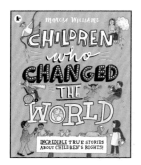

Available from all good booksellers

www.walker.co.uk